A Compilation By Best-Selling Author
DONNA IZZARD

Unstoppable Black Woman: Sisterhood Edition Volume II

© Copyright 2021 All rights reserved by Donna Izzard

All rights reserved. No part of this book may be used or reproduced in any manner whatsoever without written permission except in the case of brief quotations embodied in critical articles or reviews.

Brand It Beautifully™ Book Designs at branditbeautifully.com

ISBN: 978-0-578-34487-4

Printed in the United States of America

Table of Contents

Dedication vii

Donna Izzard 1

Atiya Boyd 7

Candaisy Patterson 15

Catherine Miles 21

Cynthia Fox Everett 27

Donna Heath-Gonzalez 33

Jeanette Grimes 39

Jiselle Alleyne-Clement 45

Maryse Nelson 53

Merolyn Rodrigues 59

Monique Johnson 67

Peshon Allen 73

Dr. Roz Knighten-Warfield 79

Tanelle Huslin 85

Tonya Twyman 91

Yolanda Davis 97

Dedication

To every Black and Brown woman and girl.
Embrace your B's and be unstoppable.

DONNA IZZARD

Unstoppable Story

Being An Unstoppable Black Woman is the sum total of many other aspects of identity, and personality, such as tenacity, resilience, the ability to understand human behavior, and other skills developed and improved through conscious choices and repetition. I have made a conscious decision that my voice as an Unstoppable Black Woman is needed for a time such as this. I recognized early on in my childhood that I had a voice that had the spirit of Harriet Tubman and Nanny (Maroon Tribe from Jamaica). I learned about the unstoppable Harriet Tubman when I was eight years old, and about the unstoppable Nanny (General in the Maroon tribe from Jamaica) as an adult. It is from these two women that I realized the power of my voice as an Unstoppable Black Woman was needed to teach others about their role as an Unstoppable Black Woman.

Black Women are some of the most misunderstood, misrepresented, unprotected, dishonored and abused creations. While many people are driven by material things and other external factors, an Unstoppable Black Woman relies on embracing her B's unapologetically – BLACK BEAUTIFUL BRILLIANT BOLD and BUSINESS-MINDED to push through. An Unstoppable Black Woman activates the daily mission of serving, sowing and supporting another Black sister.

Letter to My Younger Self

Donna, you don't have to be ashamed of your stuttering problem. I know the kids made fun of you when the teacher would call on your name, and when you stood up, the words could not come out and you would get in trouble. When the words did come, they came with a stutter. It was not your fault that no one recognized that you had a speech problem. It would have been great for someone to have sent you to speech therapy to help you with your stuttering problem. You did not know it then, but there was a great man named Moses in the Bible that stuttered as well. Just as God used Moses as a great prophet, God will use you as well. When you grow up, you won't be able to shut up because you will be speaking all over the world with the powerful voice that God gave you.

Letter to God

Dear God, Why Me?

I was only 7 years old when I used to visit my aunt for the weekend. I went out to the playground to play with my cousins and the other neighborhood children. While playing, my cousin called out to me to come and swing as well. I was only 7 years old and did not see it coming as I went towards the swings. This was in the 70s and the NYC playgrounds were all made of steel. The steel-plated swing came my way, knocking me out, and removing several of my "permanent front teeth" out of my mouth.

As I grew up as a child, I was often bullied and made fun of by my classmates, my siblings and even adults who would often ask, "what happened; why doesn't she have front teeth"? Why God? Why Me? It was not easy to hear adults and children often say, "She's cute, BUT she doesn't have any teeth in her mouth."

Write Your Own Unstoppable Letter
Dear God, Why Me?

ABOUT THE VISIONARY AUTHOR

Author, International Speaker, Women Empowerment Leader and Building Businesses God's Way, **Donna Izzard** is a woman with vision. As intuitive as she is inspirational, she helps highly successful professionals and women of faith easily become published authors to blend their expertise and brilliance into profitable, passion-fueled businesses while maintaining their full-time careers and ministries. Under Donna's tutelage and enlightening insight, her clients become more than entrepreneurs with side hustles—they become CEOpreneurs with multiple revenue streams. She is a woman with a gift.

For several years, she was the business manager for a former "White House Ambassador". As a training and development professional in the legal industry with over 30+ years of experience, she has been a mentor to women from different cultures and backgrounds. Donna was tagged as one of the top coaches to watch by the Huffington Post and most recently recognized as one of the top 30 Black Global leaders by Impact Magazine.

Connect
On the Web www.UnstoppableBlackWoman.com

ATIYA BOYD

Unstoppable Story

My innate ability to encourage, inspire and empower other women is what makes me an Unstoppable Black Woman. It's funny considering that as a young adult, I had difficulty connecting with people. It wasn't until I started working for a Social Service Agency that God revealed to me that He called me to Woman. I found that strange because I was sure that we had an understanding of how much I was willing to interact with people. He revealed it by causing a light bulb to go off in my head. As clients would come in to see me, I would always find myself ministering to them.

I would play gospel music at my desk, and it would almost always lead to a conversation about God. One of my clients came in to visit and we began to talk. She shared with me that she had only gone up to the fourth grade. I encouraged her to go back to school to get her GED. She began to cry as she proceeded to tell me that no one had ever made her feel as if she could do it. I told her that she absolutely could.

On another occasion, I had a new client come into the office. As we talked, she started telling me her reason for being at the Agency that day. She had a lot on her heart and in addition to that, she was about to lose the apartment she was living in. As she continued talking, I heard the Holy Spirit say "hug her". I did just that and she began so loud that my Colleagues came to see what was going on. About two weeks had gone by and this same client was in my office for an appointment.

She looked like a completely different person. She said, "Ms. Boyd, the day I came into your office, I felt like killing myself. When you touched me, whatever was on me lifted and I have not felt that way since." It was at that moment that I realized I had been pouring into women almost the entire time that I had been at the Agency. Who knew that the very thing that I didn't want to do turned out to be my superpower and just one of the things that makes me an Unstoppable Black Woman.

Letter to My Younger Self
Note to 16-year-old self:

Dear Atiya, you have a big future ahead of you. I want to share these nuggets with you and as simple as they may seem, they will make a tremendous difference. Always be your authentic self, the authenticity of your voice will matter, your voice is valuable, be kind to yourself, you are always a work in progress. Finally, it is perfectly ok to be different.

Note to 46-year-old self:

Dear Atiya, be kind to yourself, you are perfectly imperfect, always be your authentic self, your voice is valuable, your authenticity is necessary, don't ever shrink back, withholding the weight of what God has placed inside of you!! Always remember, that you are the daughter of The King!

Letter to God

Dear God, Why me? Who am I are the words that I uttered as I lay on the living room floor trying to pray. There was an ache in my soul that was heavier than any weight that I've ever had to bear. I have had much adversity, but this is different. This is my child!

How could you allow a stranger to almost take my son's life? I am confused and I am angry. He is not perfect, but he is a good kid that did not deserve that. How can I tell him to trust a God that would allow him to be attacked in the street in such a violent manner? What hurts the most is that right before he walked out, we had just finished praying to You. Right now, I am numb, and I need to understand how something like this could happen.

Write Your Own Unstoppable Letter
Dear God, Why Me?

ABOUT THE AUTHOR

Atiya Boyd is a Human services Professional with over 15 years of industry experience. She aspires to add value and awaken positive change by empowering women to see themselves through the lenses of God. Motivated by the drive to create a safe space for women, Atiya aims to formulate an organization where they can prosper by leveraging the power of hope to heal, restore and flourish. Atiya derives her greatest source of inspiration from helping others overcome obstacles that prevent them from becoming the best version of themselves. Attica's objective is to use her God-given ability to build a platform where women can develop solid support systems and healthy relationships. She strives to cultivate other servant leaders that understand that healthy relationships are currency.

CANDAISY PATTERSON

Unstoppable Story

Life's experiences bring about many challenges but overcoming them is what makes you an "Unstoppable Black Woman."

My journey of change began when I immigrated to the United States in 1989 with my parents and sister. After entering Junior High School, the teachers encouraged the students to speak up and project their voices. In my native Guyana, students were allowed to answer questions, but too much projection was deemed as being boastful. Writing was always my passion and I felt it was the best way for me to use my voice.

Through faith and maturity, I eventually learned how to enhance my God-given talent through speech. This didn't only benefit me, but it was a form of encouragement to other young girls and women. Using my voice gave me a sense of Boldness and Confidence. God gave me my voice and I intend to use it to spread his word and encourage others to trust and believe him, even when times seem hard.

1 Chronicles 16:11 *Seek the LORD and his strength, seek his face continually.* With God all things are possible. Go forth; Take a leap of faith; be intentional. You are an "Unstoppable Black Woman."

Letter to My Younger Self

Dear Candaisy, I would like you to follow your dreams and do not let anyone deter you. Right now, you have dreams of becoming an Interior Designer. Remember that you are able because you are making the necessary preparations to achieve this goal. God wants you to continue to serve Him because with prayer and obedience He will reward you greatly. The market that you're pursuing may not seem likely to others, but I am here to remind you to keep on pursuing what makes you happy. Do not miss your season because you choose to be different in the eyes of people. Challenges will come, but as Bishop Christopher E. Finch stated, "face your challenges with confidence." Hold on to God's promises and remember that you are "Unstoppable."

Letter to God

Heavenly Father, I come before You humbly, and I thank You for Your grace and mercy. Father, You promised that You will never leave me nor forsake me, and I hold on to these promises. One thing that I know is that being obedient to You allows me to hear Your voice clearer. Having "Prayer Board Meetings" with You enables me to pay keen attention to Your instructions. Lord, I thank You for guiding my path and shielding me from danger seen and unseen. I will continue to be uplifted and encouraged by Your promises. I pray Psalm 91:4 daily as a constant reminder of who You are to me. Amen.

Write Your Own Unstoppable Letter
Dear God, Why Me?

ABOUT THE AUTHOR

Candaisy Patterson is a wife and mother to three kings and one princess. She was born in Georgetown, Guyana and migrated to the United States in 1989. Candaisy currently resides in Brooklyn, NY. Candaisy did her high school education in Queens, NY. She continued her education and graduated with her BS in TV/Radio with Advertising and Market from Brooklyn College. Candaisy currently works at a major US airline during the day and she is also the CEO at Premiere Events & Designs, Inc. Her passion for Christ is a driving force in Candaisy's life and she serves in several ministries at Hope for All Outreach Christian Center. She continues to improve her education through advanced-learning courses.

Email: Candaisypatterson@gmail.com | Premiereevents.designs@gmail.com

IG: @premiere_events_design

CATHERINE MILES

Unstoppable Story

I am an unstoppable black woman because I have been able to navigate through every obstacle that has been put in front of me. For every door that was closed by the enemy, God gave me a key to open it. Every stumbling block that the enemy used to trip me up was used by God to build me up. The mere fact that my voice can speak through these words and pages proves that I AM UNSTOPPABLE! My UNSTOPPABLE BLACK WOMAN voice is needed for a time such as this.

Letter to My Younger Self

Hey, dear little girl Catherine. I know it's kind of lonely on the playground by yourself. I want you to know that before I formed you, I knew you. I purposely put your mom in your dad's pathway so that you could be created. I know you don't understand now because it's too much for your mind to comprehend at this time. Catherine, you will go through some rough times as a child and be forced into adulthood at a very young age. I want you to know that when mother and father forsake you, I will still be there. When those you trust turn their backs on you, I will still be there. Catherine, you have learned how to survive and how to take care of yourself at a very young age. This doesn't make sense right now but, as you get older, you will understand. Always remember this YOU HAVE VALUE, YOU ARE WORTH IT ALL! People will try and lie to you and bring up your childhood, but remember, THAT'S A LIE. The devil is the father of LIES. He will try to trick you and make you think you're not worth saving. I AM your father, and I will never leave nor forsake you! YOU HAVE VALUE!

Letter to God

For most of my life, I've asked the question, "GOD WHY ME?" It seemed as if He never answered until now at the age of 56; He replied and said, "Why not you?" When people put me on trial and ask if God is real, I want my best witness on the stand to testify on my behalf. Catherine, you have always been My particular star witness. I was there and watched you abandoned as a baby and placed in a foster home. I even watched you be set back with your natural family only to be rejected. I watched you go through alcohol, drugs, and even physical abuse so that you could feel like you belonged to something or someone, but it only numbed you. I've watched you go through cancer treatment alone as you covered up your pain. I remember you saying, "God must hate me."

Even through all of this, you still called Me ABBA Father. I knew I could put you on the stand to speak on my behalf. You would say yes, "HE IS GOD." Catherine, you are the apple of My eye. I knew they couldn't break you. You are that unstoppable, fearfully and wonderfully made woman. You are brave despite it all. Even not knowing what was ahead, it never stopped you. You still pursued Me. You are relentless, bold, and beautiful, and nothing could prevent you from getting to Me. This is why YOU! Your love for My love and Me for you will never change your look like your DADDY GOD!

Write Your Own Unstoppable Letter
Dear God, Why Me?

ABOUT THE AUTHOR

Catherine Miles, educator and mother of three, Christopher, Kennedy-and Caleb, and one five-year-old grandson's proud grandmother. Currently working in Education K-5 grade. Has also served in pivotal roles in ministry, from directing choir to teaching Sunday to her current role as a Culture Specialist at All Nations Worship Assembly providing resources and setting standards for serving teams in volunteering. Catherine is an advocate for the community, giving voice to inequities -her greatest joy is helping others.

CYNTHIA FOX EVERETT

Unstoppable Story

I never thought I would be the one to break the generational curses of mental illness, alcoholism domestic violence, suicide, poverty, teenage pregnancy, divorce, rape, molestation, and addiction. No, I didn't ask for it but I have risen to the occasion. God blessed me with four children and eight grandchildren and more to follow. I know that the pain of staying in a dead barren place is more painful than death itself. I'm their link to salvation to a flourishing legacy of love and knowing the Lord and forgiveness. Teaching them that pain propels not paralyzes. That with God all things are possible if we just have faith. That you can cry, wipe your tears, and get up at the same time. Reassuring them that some mountains God will move them but others you have to ask God for the strength to climb! That He uses everything that we do in our lives, even the mistakes. We aren't perfect and we are going to make mistakes and fall down but remember not to stay there. My pain and disappointments haven't broken me thus far. I use them as a platform for my next level of happiness and success! I've learned to find the silver lining in every rainstorm. I know that when I win everything attached to me wins and that quitting has never been an option. Yes, they do see me cry but they also see me rejoice! I am unstoppable! The pain stops here.

Letter to My Younger Self

First, I'm very proud of the strength, courage, and responsibility that you have at a young age. With all you have survived, don't forget to replace bitterness, stagnation, anger, and resentment with plenty of forgiveness of self and others, self-love and self-acceptance. Don't forget to dash a lot of compassion on top of it all like Jesus did. Remember to always seek and keep God first and develop a lifelong relationship with Him. Worth isn't earned by others but it's an inherited birthright. Forgiving and the act of forgiveness go hand in hand. Don't forget to show grace and mercy into your own soul. You will eventually get to live your YES just hold on. God knows all and sees all. Know that you aren't a victim but a survivor, a warrior and you will live and not die! I love and cherish and honor you!

Letter to God

Dear God Why Me? Why was I chosen to break the generational curses of mental illness, poverty, alcoholism and domestic violence; to care for my mother and raise my grandchildren?

Black-My blackness is like a rare black pearl that's priceless and powerful.

Beautiful-My beauty radiates confidence and I love myself unconditionally.

Brilliant-My brilliance allows me to pursue and overtake all of my goals and dreams effectively.

Bold-I am bold when I speak and communicate how I feel and how others treat me.

Business-Minded-I believe that my gifts and talents allow me to be successful in my business.

Write Your Own Unstoppable Letter
Dear God, Why Me?

_____

_____

_____

_____

_____

_____

_____

_____

_____

_____

_____

_____

_____

_____

_____

_____

_____

_____

_____

_____

_____

_____

_____

_____

_____

ABOUT THE AUTHOR

Cynthia Fox Everett is a mother of four, grandmother of eight. She is a U.S. Army veteran of fourteen years. She has an associate degree in Criminal Justice and furthered her education at Shaw University. She rededicated her life to Christ in 2003 and accepted the mission and the responsibility to serve in the house of the Lord. She wants to empower and inspire others to seek Jesus and find the strength to heal so that they dare to rewrite their future, tell their story, and help others heal. She is also a certified life coach and a

Multimulti-Bestselling Co-Author author of Amazon's Souled Out and Souled Out Volumne 2, Soul Talk, Volume 2, Soul Talk, Volume 3 and Soulful Affirmations with Cheryl Polote- Williamson as the visionary. She is also a bestselling Co-author with visionary Venessa D. Abram, MBA, in "The Voices Behind Mental. Illness, Series 2," The Life of a Soldier, Series 5 and a bestselling Co-author with visionary, Donna Izzard in "The Unstoppable Black Woman, The Sisterhood Edition". She is an advocate for domestic violence and a survivor, also a Mental Health/survivor/ advocate.

To connect email her at cynthiaeverett8@gmail.com

DONNA HEATH-GONZALEZ

Unstoppable Story

The road to entrepreneurship highlights success, growth, longevity, challenges, perseverance, amongst others. Experiencing these highlights allows me to pursue my God-given purpose and passion while serving others. When the path to your purpose is a vision from God, you can persevere along with it unapologetically.

As an Unstoppable Black Woman persevering in the beauty supply industry for over a decade is truly a blessing even though challenges are present. Nevertheless, with determination, I continued embracing "B" s unapologetically by being Black, Bold, Beautiful, Brave, and Business-Minded, which allows me to serve, sow, teach and pave the path for other my unstoppable sisters.

Not having prior experience in this sector of the beauty industry, which is known to be one of the most challenging sectors for us to succeed in, did not deter me from the vision to be present and unstoppable.

My vision was born during the 2008 recession when I opened my first store. I've grown to two stores and an online store with its warehouse space with God's grace, perseverance, success, and longevity.

Fast forward now in 2020, my vision was tested as we all experienced the COVID 19 pandemic and was temporarily closed for our safety. However, this downtime was still a journey along my path, which taught me that pivoting towards my purpose does not take away from me an Unstoppable Black Woman. On the contrary, it indeed encourages, motivates, and inspires me to continue embracing my "B" s unapologetically.

Letter to My Younger Self
Dear Self:

The one thing that I know now and wish I knew then is to say NO and not feel bad about it. As children, we were taught to be kind, respectful, and caring. I do believe in those qualities because they have helped shape the woman I have grown to become.

Looking back through different stages of my younger years made me realize that saying NO is not unkind, disrespectful, or less caring. The truth is, it allows me to set boundaries, keep out distractions and negativity, which contributes to hurt.

Knowing that the past cannot be changed, staying there will hinder me from growing to become a voice for herself and others.

The beauty of this self-reflection is that it's teaching me that people will treat you the way they want to if you allow them to.

My takeaway, I will be at peace saying NO at any stage of my life.

Letter to God

Dear God, Why Me? God, you have given me the strength to overcome many of life's challenges, yet as I am in the midst of them, I find myself having to forget about mine to see others through theirs.

Why Me God? - I am neither a therapist nor a counsellor but yet my desire to be attentive, listen and encourage others, coupled with the caring heart you have blessed me with, taught me that you have created me for more.

Why Me God? - God, I thank you for walking me through my life's challenges because through it all, you have chosen me to execute your orders as I sow, serve and support others. Glory to You, God!

Write Your Own Unstoppable Letter
Dear God, Why Me?

ABOUT THE AUTHOR

Donna Heath-Gonzalez, long time owner of Big Apple Beauty Supply stores in Northeast Pennsylvania. Leaving a career in accounting in 2008, she grew from a flea market stand to two large stores that expanded multiple times. Big Apple Beauty Supply stood out from the other retailers in the industry because it was rooted in the relationships and respect formed between the patrons and Big Apple Beauty team. It was a priority to collaborate with patrons to find the products that were just right for them.

Connect: babshair.com

JEANETTE GRIMES

Unstoppable Story

I AM Jeanette. I have accepted that I am the daughter of The One, The Only, Most High, Living God. Big Daddy for real.

I am forever grateful to my high school sweetheart for five amazing blessings called children. Once upon a time, I was single-parenting and surviving. I then decided to thrive. It was a decision, a declaration and dedication to do: a personal mission. I work. I mean I work! I love my children, they proved to me, even more, that God is the lover of my soul and He is real.

During life, I have been blind-sided by the unbelievable. I have been helped by the unexpected. God told me, convinced me, and showed me: HE is always with me and will never leave me. God has proved Himself over and over through tithing of my life: time, talent and treasury notes. When I learned that God the Father, God the Son and God the Holy Spirit wanted a relationship with me and wanted the best for me, I became unabashedly unstoppable. Because of God, I am enveloped in relentless love.

I will remain unstoppable for all my children, my grandchildren, family, community and enemies. I will remain unstoppable by any means necessary: emotions, mind, body, soul, and spirit. I live in God and He lives in my heart. I declare, from my bones to His throne, by the grace of God, all of me is unstoppable.

Letter to My Younger Self

Hey Lillie's Girl!

Keep following the Word of God. You have to keep moving forward regardless of others who may not be moving forward in life. You don't have to shrink back because others are insecure. God said, be strong! Press on into your God-given purpose. God gave you a voice, use it. Stay healthy in your mind, body and soul. Watch for subtle, sneak attacks on your mind, body, soul and emotions. Keep smiling, keep singing, keep dancing, keep praising, and keep praying everywhere you go. Your body is a temple, a glorious temple. You are here for a tremendous purpose, run on purpose. Remember what Lillie told you, "Choose who you gon' be and be that person, so people know who they' gettin'." Remember: NEVER be lacking in ZEAL or spiritual fervor serving the LORD (Romans 12:11 NIV).

Letter to God

Dear God, Why Me? God, Thank You, for continuously letting me know 'why' while working for me, with me and in me. You let me know through Romans 8: 28 that all things work together to the good of them that love the Lord. I believe God. Romans 8:28 kept and keeps me grounded in knowing after the situation, You will work it for my good, even when it did not look or feel good to my situation, my emotions or my heart.

My Affirmation: I am created for Helpful Information Sharing, While Inspiring Lifelong Learning, Motivating, Educating and Training.

Write Your Own Unstoppable Letter
Dear God, Why Me?

ABOUT THE AUTHOR

Jeanette Grimes is a vibrant and motivating sharer of Good News! Jeanette loves to encourage others. She describes herself as a Jersey girl with Virginia flavor. She earned her Master's degree in Human Services from Lincoln University in 2010. Jeanette is an entrepreneur: author of the Journal: Decide Declare Do, she is the founder of LEZEAL Enterprises, LLC and creator of The Good News Newsletter.

Jeanette loves to laugh and aims to make others smile. She places the highest priority on her relationship with God, family and serving the community for Kingdom purposes. She has five biological children, bonus non-biological children and an abundance of grandchildren. Jeanette is grateful for each opportunity to help communities and families. She expresses her gratitude for being part of positive world change. She thanks God, her family, friends and Kingdom co-workers for supporting her in her Kingdom-building endeavors.

Jiselle Alleyne-Clement

Unstoppable Story

"We can't be afraid of change. You may feel very secure in the pond that you are in, but if you never venture out of it, you will never aknow that there is such a thing as an ocean..." ~ C. Joy Bell

I have learnt a lot of lessons from my journey of self-discovery. Many people are afraid to begin a journey of self-discovery because they are afraid of the 'self' they may find and even more afraid of the task of developing the true 'self' they were created to be. The task is a daunting one, but the journey of self-discovery forces us to first put our lives in the hands of our Heavenly Father, and it forces us to declare like the psalmist David, 'Search me O God and know my heart, try me and know my anxieties and see if there be any wicked way in me...' (Psalm 139: 23-24).

Marianne Williamson stated that "It takes courage to endure the sharp pains of self-discovery..." and so at the age of forty, I summoned courage and began my journey. A successful career that had taken me grit and force to build was crumbling before my very eyes, and I stopped 'living'. I lived like a zombie, going through the motions outside, but lifeless on the inside. I lived my life wearing a myriad of masks, concealing the truth, from myself and others. But, at age forty, I surrendered to the process, I chose to embark upon self-discovery.

And so began my isolation period, I called it the isolation chamber. I began the journey of stripping off the masks. It was a painful, solitary, but necessary time. When my isolation period ended, I was able, for the first time, to look in the mirror and appreciate the woman God had made, fearfully and wonderfully made, knowing her worth in Christ and most of all 'free'.

Letter to My Younger Self

Matthew 13:45-46 The Voice (VOICE)

The kingdom of heaven is like a jeweller on the lookout for the finest pearls. When he found a pearl more beautiful and valuable than any jewel he had ever seen, the jeweller sold all he had and bought that pearl, his pearl of great price

Dear Jissy,

On your journey of Self-Discovery, you will discover that you are a precious pearl. Know that a single pearl takes years to cultivate and so take your time, don't rush the 'formation' process. Understand that you are very valuable, and each life experience adds to your value, for the value of a pearl is timeless, and it never depreciates. You will also realise that there is no perfect pearl, but every imperfection adds to the beauty of the pearl and increases its value in the eyes of the beholder.

So, my dear Jissy, stand in your uniqueness, for no two pearls are alike, which makes you the highly prized gem you are. Allow yourself the freedom to add to the world your unique expression.

And as you blossom into the fullness of your womanhood, don't let comparison with another pearl impede you on your journey of self-discovery.

Jiselle Alleyne-Clement

Letter to God

Dear God, My life has taken another twist, sending me into the middle of another Transition. I feel like Abraham when you told him to leave and go to a land that you will 'show' him. Well, God, I have obeyed, but I am still waiting to see the land, and while I am waiting, the trials seem like they are my best friends. God, I have been down this road before, but I thought I would not have to take this journey again at this time in my life. But even as I walk through uncharted territory, I will remember that you want me to walk with hinds' feet, and fly like an eagle.

AFFIRMATION:

I am a BEAUTIFUL daughter of the most-high, BOLD as a Lioness, and you will hear me roar as I walk into my wealthy place.

Write Your Own Unstoppable Letter
Dear God, Why Me?

ABOUT THE AUTHOR

Jiselle Alleyne-Clement is a professional of many hats. She is an Academic Librarian, Educator and Researcher. She received her MLIS in Library Science from Dalhousie University, Canada. She also holds an MA in Leadership Studies from the University of Guelph, Canada, and she is currently reading for her PhD in Gender Studies at the University of the West Indies, focusing on Female Leadership Development in Caribbean Organisations.

Jiselle is the lead Empowerment Speaker, Vision Coach and Mentor, through her consultancy, 'Pearls of Great Price Empowerment Services', a consultancy developed for faith-based women.

The empowerment programmes offered through her consultancy are geared to help women manage the transitions in their lives and will treat with topics such as, but not limited to:

- Competencies for Seamless Transition Management

- Establishing Healthy and Productive SHE Team Cultures

- SHE Leadership Development

- Developing a Resilience Mindset

Jiselle believes that every woman must be given access to this type of development where she can, in turn, lead within her sphere of influence.

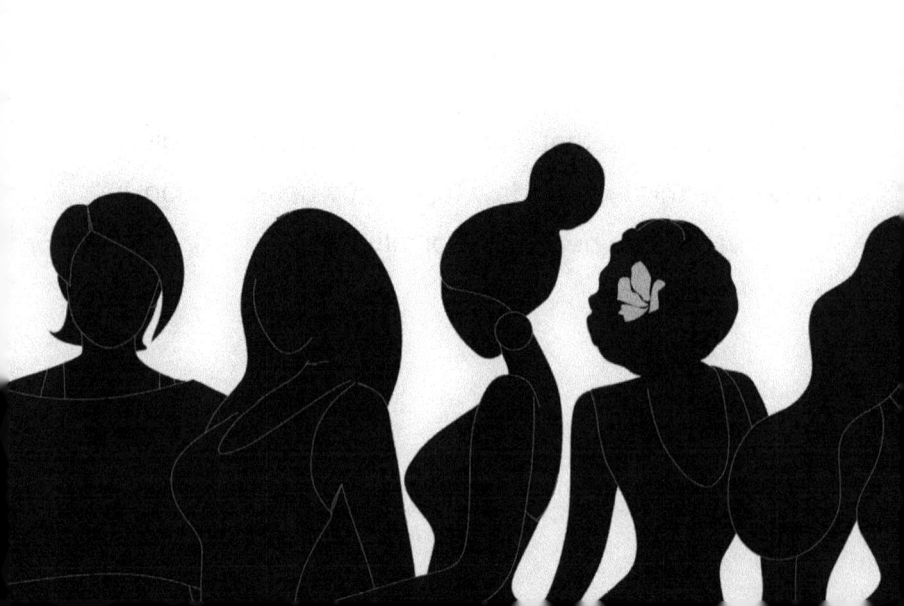

MARYSE NELSON

Unstoppable Story

I call them "great big things" that invite themselves into our lives. Some are amazing blessings, but most actually crash in, with no other intention but to kill and destroy. One day, in perfect evil character, one such thing paid me an unannounced visit. It slaughtered my very productive, Florida-sun-kissed dream of life! With meticulous precision, betrayal struck with a vengeance and landed me, headfirst, into the ashes of despair. It was powerful, sly, intelligent, and it tore me to pieces. It demolished my perfect foundation.

That day, I was informed that life, as I knew it, would come to a painful, screeching halt. My marriage would not survive. I was convinced it was the end-- So great was the fear, so devastating the humiliation! God, however, stood up bigger and spoke up louder! Today, victoriously, I stand on His promises, training, leading, speaking against the very thing that came to destroy me.

My unstoppable voice is necessary because ordinary days are being pummeled by evil, 'great big things' everywhere in our world. Women are reeling helplessly, as the sacred monuments of their lives, their dreams, are imploding into piles of debris. Their spirits are being crushed, but in the middle of the rubble, they will hear my voice! God has made me an authority on the subject of their pain. It is my assignment to teach them how to transform those evil, 'great big things' into powerful tools for the Kingdom of God. I boldly stand and accept the challenge!

Letter to My Younger Self

Hey girl, I am so proud of you! I love your attitude; your big innocent heart; your love for people, especially underdogs. You fluidly navigate around chaos and always find your way, relying mostly on your faith. I am super proud of you! A few words of caution, though: The day is coming when people will blatantly try you, hurt you, insult you. Some will abandon you altogether. You will face many dark days ahead. Sometimes you will spend yourself a lot, but you will not get any reward, not even justice. Don't worry, you will be fine. Spend very little time crying about it, it's not worth it!

Now I know God will always work things right for your improvement. Appreciate the fullness of life: your beautiful, shameful, easy, impossible, wicked, angelic mélange of realities. You are phenomenal! Keep working for the Kingdom. I love you dearly.

Letter to God

Dear God, I love You. I am grateful for Your many blessings, but there's something I'd really like to know: why me? Why, in Your plans for me, did You include so much shame? Why is my assignment the cross I most despise? I don't question Your will. I accept it but still, I am curious. What qualified me for this job? I know the answer will light my soul on fire.

As my ancestors' dream, I am Bold!

I am ten blazing suns, Beautiful, Brilliant!

I ride with panthers, independent, Black!

I am a success, Business-minded!

I am an Unstoppable Black Woman!

Write Your Own Unstoppable Letter
Dear God, Why Me?

ABOUT THE AUTHOR

Maryse Nelson wears many hats. She is the founder and president of Samarita Global Outreach, a 501 (C3) nonprofit organization. They are active in the US, Haiti, and the Dominican Republic. Flagship programs include FANM KAJOU (Women Ministry), SUPERCHAMPS (Youth Leadership Program) and XL-Care (Elderly/Senior Program).

Maryse is available as a Professional Speaker and Certified Life Coach Minister. She holds a Physical

Therapy degree from NYU and an MBA from the University of Phoenix.

As an author, her books include: Second to None (For home health professionals), From the Ashes: Lessons We Learn, and Renaitre de ses Cendres.

As an Insurance Broker, Maryse enjoys serving the public at C&J One-Stop Services/ MNC.

She is the host of "Plus Haut Plus Loin" (Aiming Higher and Farther), a weekly motivational program on Radio Esperans, broadcasting in the United States and Haiti. Maryse also hosts the Master Thinkers and Movers podcast on Anchor and Spotify.

IG: @mnelson_samaritaglobal

www.mysamarita.com

info@choosenelson.com

MEROLYN RODRIGUES

Unstoppable Story

My purposeful God is always with me and because of Him, I am unstoppable. His presence through the Holy Spirit is something that I am so greatly for. It is greater than any troubles I encounter, obstacles in my path, or situations I may face. It brings healing and joy.

His guidance has helped me navigate through the trauma of the loss of family members and friends, knowing what to do when I do not.

He never ceases to amaze me with always being on time. Always knowing what I need when I need it.

Connecting with Him in prayer and speaking in my heavenly language allow us to communicate on an unexplainable level. I learned how to trust and turn to His promises in times of challenging situations.

I meditate on His word and develop a deeper relationship with Him where I have grown spiritually. His peace is far more wonderful than the human mind can comprehend; it is really a peace that surpasses all understanding.

His signs through dreams speak of things to come and when I reach out to Him, He tells me of unsearchable things that I would not be able to grasp without Him.

I seek Him first and I know that through Him and with Him, I can do all things. I have been and will continue to be unstoppable

Letter to My Younger Self
Dear younger self, I pray for you to have self-realization and the discernment to know that "You will become the thing you think about the most".

Watch your thoughts, never let anyone tell you that you cannot achieve what you desire or want to accomplish in life. Surround yourself with friends who have your best interest at heart.

Have goals, visualize, and write down things that the small voice tells you. Repeat positive affirmations daily and stand on God's never-changing promises. Stand until they become reality.

You are destined for greatness, so stay focused and when you need a break, take one, refuel and begin again.

Pray without ceasing for guidance. Stand firm in faith and believe that you can achieve your heart's desire.

Never be too hard on yourself; always do your best and work as unto the Lord. Be grateful for each new day to be unstoppable.

Letter to God

Dear God, At the age of 12, I remember asking you why me? I was traumatized after witnessing my father's passing. My body and soul hurt. He was my rock, the kindest person I knew; the father who was always there for me.

Now, I have stopped asking that question, instead, I say, "why not me?"

For with each test, I turned to You, Father, I grew spiritually, learned, experienced Your love, and have testimonies.

My testimonies allow me to be a witness to others when they are going through trials.

I am BOLD and I will not apologize for being royal, knowing the woman I am in Christ, and declaring Your promise daily.

Write Your Own Unstoppable Letter
Dear God, Why Me?

ABOUT THE AUTHOR

Merolyn Rodrigues is an accountant by day for one of the top financial institutions in the world. She is also the CEO of HTTS Floral and Event Designs located in New York. A certified luxury floral designer and event planner who provides services for all occasions. As a creative designer, she curates memorable luxury experiences worldwide. "This Heir to God's seed", transforms space into magical, inspiring moments. Creating trendy, lush bridal bouquets, and large Extravagant designs of fresh and silk flowers is a promise. Continuously investing in educating herself in floral and event design while building her skillsets for the floral industry.

Merolyn's work was featured in the Munaluchi Bride Magazine Summer Edition 2021.

Contact Merolyn on Instagram and Facebook

@httsfloralandeventdesign

merolyn@httsfloral.com

www.httsfloralandeventdesign

MONIQUE JOHNSON

Unstoppable Story

I am black, bold, and a believer! I went from being a 19-year-old single mother on public assistance to a six-figure income earner! I came to a crossroad early in life when I found myself on a curb at 2 am in my pajamas contemplating what to do next. It was my first year in college, away from home, and no place to stay. My headstrong, "I'm grown," attitude led me there. I had a decision to make: stay and struggle, or leave and start again. I left the four-year university to attend a community college back home. The best decision I could have made. You see, eight weeks later, I learned I was pregnant. I refused to become another young black girl with a baby, not married, and on welfare. I reassessed, made some adjustments, and set new goals.

Thank God for my unstoppable black mother! She helped me get a job and kept my son while I went to school at night. I graduated with my AA in Business Management, and later a BS in Business Administration. Today, I am a high-income earner and a homeowner. I was relentless about overcoming. For any woman who has gone through setbacks, decide to be relentless in your pursuits.

Letter to My Younger Self

Dear Little Nikki, walk with your head held high. This is the posture of confidence. A very nice man gave me that advice when I was 12 years old. Confidence will take you far. Be aware of people who say they are friends, but will foolishly bring pain and humiliation into your life. When that happens, remember the first thing I said; hold your head up. Walk away leaving them and the situation behind you. Do not give it your energy. It will only consume you. People hurt one another intentionally, or unintentionally. Choose to forgive, and do not take anything personal. Keep God first. Be relentless in your pursuits.

Letter to God

Dear God, why me? Lord, You know that I've had my share of struggles. I trusted you through the breast cancer and overcame. I've been through a divorce, lost two homes, and had co-workers try to break me, but I prevailed because of You. Now, I carry the burdens of my children, friends, and some co-workers. This, by far, is harder. Dear God, why me? Why am I the one that people reach out to for encouragement? I don't have a perfect life. My first-born son joined a gang as a pre-teen, and was sentenced to 12 years in prison, though no one was hurt, or shot? Why did this happen even though I lived as an example by getting my degrees, working good-paying jobs, and putting him in a Christian school? Why is my daughter struggling with anxiety? Why does my middle son lack motivation? Lord, I believe I know the answer, it is because of who I am; a relentless, Bold Black Woman who stands in the gap for those who cannot stand for themselves.

Write Your Own Unstoppable Letter
Dear God, Why Me?

ABOUT THE AUTHOR

Monique Johnson is a bold and brilliant daughter of God. She is a mother of three, grandmother of two, and a relentless overcomer. Monique elevated from a 19-year-old single mother on public assistance to a six-figure earner! She breaks strongholds and inspires others to do the same. Monique has a heart for young mothers and wayward sons. She formed a nonprofit after-school program to help keep teens off of the streets and brought awareness to the Prison Industrial Complex that was created to keep the minority population incarcerated. She mentored youth to keep them from making bad choices that could land them in the unforgiving criminal justice system. Monique is a senior project manager in the aerospace industry, and has a gift of teaching and coaching men and women in business, personal, and spiritual development.

Email: monique2956@gmail.com

Instagram - @envision.1t

Facebook - Monique Johnson

PESHON ALLEN

Unstoppable Story

"For I have known the thoughts that I am thinking towards you -- an affirmation of Jehovah; thoughts of peace, and not of evil, to give to you posterity and hope."
~ Jeremiah 29:11 – YLT

Growing up on the west side of Chicago in Henry Horner projects wasn't easy; in fact, it was dangerous! But I would not change a thing. It was during those times that I saw God protecting my Mother, a single Mom with three kids growing up in the "hood." Growing up in that environment, you feel hopeless and that your "story", and your life will not have a good ending. I always had to fight. Fight to prove myself, fight to protect myself from people trying to do harm to a little girl. Years later, as an adult, I was still fighting and didn't know why. Until, one day The Lord said to me, "Peshon, you don't have to fight anymore." And I felt He was saying, let me fight for you and it's okay to put your guard down. When you go through years of this, you feel like you're not good enough for anything or anybody. However, with God's word, I finally realized that I am not a product of my past, but a product of His Word that I apply to my life, and with Him, I have hope and a future. God was not going to abandon me like my earthly father. I could now help others to tell their story and have hope for the future God created them for. God was with me and He is giving me hope, peace and prosperity. He just wanted to know if I would believe and trust Him for it.

Letter to My Younger Self

Listen to me and listen well. You are enough. You are beautiful. You are anointed. You are everything that God created you to be NOW, Own it, possess it and walk in it. Time isn't waiting on you, it is a gift to you, USE IT. Maximize all the time given to you, because once it is gone, you can't get it back. Maximize all your gifts. Stop doubting yourself. Believe and Know. Agree with God for your life. Know that God is for you. He is on your side. You will not fail. Do every creative and witty idea God has given you to do. Waste no time! Remember, pour into your children, they are your legacy. Pour everything out and die empty. But in the meantime, live life to the fullest and enjoy it! On your mark, get ready and You Are Ready Girl. It's yours, now GO! I am an Unstoppable Black Woman.

Letter to God

Father God, I thank You for my life and for always being there for me. There is never a time I can remember You not being there, guiding and protecting me from danger. I love You, Father God because when my earthly father abandoned me, You picked me up and always provided for me. Through all the pain and rejection, You have always been Consistent. I owe You my life. You are my everything. Lord, You are my Light. I Believe You. I have Faith in You always. With everything that I am, I love You Father, Your Daughter Forever.

Write Your Own Unstoppable Letter
Dear God, Why Me?

ABOUT THE AUTHOR

Peshon Allen is a servant and believer in Jesus Christ, a Wife, Mother, Worship Leader, and Speaker. She is a Bestselling Co-Author, an Army Veteran, an alumnus of American Forces Network and a licensed minister.

Peshon is the Founder behind the podcast called, "Women In Ministry On The Move-NOW!" A very popular online radio show that empowers women from all walks of life and services they provide in ministry and their communities.

Peshon is married to the love of her life, Mr. Tyron Allen of 21 years, and shares two beautiful children. Born in Chicago, she quickly learned that education and pit-bull tenacity were key to a better life. She holds a Bachelor's Degree in Theology, with Honors, from Minnesota Graduate Bible College and a second Bachelor's in Communications and Journalism. Her motto is, "All Things are Possible with GOD, just believe, and Trust the Lord.

Connect on Facebook @Peshonallen

Website www.peshonallen.com

DR. ROZ KNIGHTEN-WARFIELD

Unstoppable Story

I've gone through life believing that I was a hot chocolate fudge sundae mess until I was blessed with new girlfriends that were purposed & positioned by God that I've met since the age of 50. Now don't take this the wrong way before fifty peeps. My unstoppable B is being **BLACK** and check out the acronym that credit goes to the higher source of **El Shaddai**, the **God of more than enough**:

Beloved
Live
Always
Conquering
Kindness

I AM, a **Beloved** daughter that will **Live** for **Always Conquering** biblical **Kindness**. **BLACK** is my **unstoppable B and I'm sticking to the answer**. This season I have truly learned that relational currency is queen, no pun intended. I've been blessed that when

I could not see the greatness and brilliance in myself that there were sistahs who loved me and looked beyond my faults seeking for the precious gems of true friendship. I love, appreciate, celebrate, value and most cherish the efforts that I have learned to truly understand, I am my sistahs keeper!

Sisterhood is a precious commodity and when you are willing to love, learn, lead and stop the lies of self condemnation, then your light shines brightly and it attracts others. These women come bearing their authentic selves and carried an ethical code of honesty, integrity and character. These women know that cultivation is key and respect is high on the list to garner one another's perspective. My unstoppable **BLACK!** I AM MY SISTAHS KEEPER! **#MoreThanEnough**

Letter to My Younger Self

The bullying, the teasing, the mocking and more! Who taught children to treat other children badly and before that the memories of being molested. Life is a sho nuff trip and it does not make sense to pay for excessive baggage when you don't even wear it all on the trip. Metaphorically, I am talking about all the jammed packed lies that were encoded in my head that I was not pretty enough, I had short hair, I was not light enough, I stuttered, and the last one to complete the test. Through the years this made me feel inadequate.

Well let's go into a supernatural editing mode. Baby girl you are the apple of His eye. You are more than enough. You have greatness and brilliance inside. Your potential is ready to bust loose so make a clear runway. Refuel, Replenish and Recharge It's Your Season! Arise, Black, Bold, Beautiful, Brilliant, and Business-minded women, #Reset In Jesus name Amen!

Letter to God

This is the day that the Lord has made and I will rejoice and be glad in it! Psalm 118:24. Lord, you know me well. You have my back and it's time to own my authority as a child of a mighty KING! I am willing and no longer hold myself hostage due to lies of myself and the world. Jehovah Chayil is my favorite God name. I shall reign in worship, wisdom, wealth, power, virtue, honor, favor, influence and an army rising up! In Jesus Name Amen!

Write Your Own Unstoppable Letter
Dear God, Why Me?

ABOUT THE AUTHOR

Dr. Roz Knighten-Warfield is a Smilepreneur and founder of Roz Knighten-Warfield Enterprises, certified coach, Amazon best selling international author, public speaker and known as the smile genius. Roz teaches relational currency, collaborative measures, effective partnerships and covenant agreements to "SMILE": Simply Make Intentional Love Encounters, starting with oneself first. Roz is a prayer warrior who is passionate about connecting with successful partners with vision, men and women who are leaders and are willing to bring others alongside them. When you work with Roz, she will show you how to "SOAR" like an eagle into your divine calling. Be surrendered, obedient, abiding radically for kingdom sake. She says you are loved, appreciated, celebrated, valued and most cherished! Her favorite scripture is Psalms 119:35 Smile on me, your servant: teach me the right way to live. MSG

Email: roz@rozknightenwarfield.com

Website: rozknightenwarfield.com

TANELLE HUSLIN

Unstoppable Story

There was a time in my life when I was silent. I had a unique voice, but it didn't allow me to fit in; sometimes, I would alter my pitch and speak. However, I would use that voice louder in my prayer time with God. As I grew up and accomplished some of my life goals, I felt empty and stuck. I know there was much more from within.

In 2019, I was about to journey to a destination with a major career shift. I had a conversation with God whom I choose to be my guide and that's when His promise in Psalm 32:8 was activated. During that time, I was quickened to use my inner voice, which I pursued but minimally. In 2021, God guided me to a platform where I had to decide to raise my hand and speak. Little did I know, this was an open door with many opportunities, ones that allow me to share my story as a co-author. I realized that ears and hearts were waiting to hear what I had to say. This was when I acknowledged that the little I kept saying availed much because I was empowered by God. I started to speak up and out whatever God placed inside of me. The more I say, the further I go; my purpose and destiny are clearer. I am walking through more effective doors as they were already opened just waiting for me. I started to experience fulfillment, not knowing that my evolution was silenced because I was silent. I am UNSTOPPABLE.

Letter to My Younger Self

Hey Girl Hey! I am so proud of you, listen to me well. Please be extremely grateful and embrace everything that life's journey has to offer. The good, bad, discomfort, obstacles, challenges, lessons, and opportunities because they all work together for your good says your Father. His plans and purpose for you are good and not evil. Remember when you felt weird and wanted to rebel because you couldn't do what everyone was doing. You are a bright light peculiarly created, who had to be different to shine. I wish you had appreciated it more. Nonetheless, now that you know, in your uniqueness, you are **B**old with your **B**rilliance and **B**eauty as you cultivate your **B**usiness mind for God's kingdom. God is always with you on this journey; not once did he take his eyes off you. Gods' goodness is chasing you down as you grow, you are abundantly blessed.

Letter to God

Father, I praise You for who You are and Your mighty works in my life. I'm grateful for the assignment and orders You choose me for on this earth. Lord, I'm curious **WHY ME?** Am I worthy and deserving of such grace? What I see is so much bigger than me. Lord, am I capable and qualified for this? With all these questions I have, Lord I know my sister reading now has questions too. Thank you for answering this prayer that I can solemnly affirm I am **B**old; I am **L**oved, I can do **A**ll things through **C**hrist who strengthens me. I **C**elebrate and give myself permission to evolve and build up God's **K**ingdom.

Write Your Own Unstoppable Letter
Dear God, Why Me?

ABOUT THE AUTHOR

Tanelle Huslin, is a chosen woman and lover of God and His people. She has a passion to inspire, motivate and encourage individuals of the hope in pressing as they journey forward in life.

As a born and raised Jamaican, now living in the United States, she had to undergo some major system changes that push her further to her purpose. A budding entrepreneur of Festivi-T World (Jamaica) & 4wardbyFaith LLC, she pursued her Bachelors in

Business Administration and currently performs duties as a Personal Banker.

Tanelle expands on her inner drive as a prayer warrior while using the authority given by God to stand on His words. She desires that God will use her as a willing vessel to ignite and uplift people through prayers, testimonies and power-working words of affirmations as they go forward by what Jesus said "**Have faith in God" Mark 11:22.**

Tanelle is a devoted mother to a young king Tejean. Please Stay Tuned.

Instagram & Facebook: @4wardbyfaith

YouTube: 4wardbyfaith

Email: 4wardbyfaith@gmail.com

TONYA TWYMAN

Unstoppable Story

On May 10, 2003, two police officers stood at my door and asked me if I was Mrs. Reed and I said yes. They spoke these words that changed my life forever: "Mrs. Reed we regret to inform you that your husband was a victim of a homicide in Los Angeles California last night". We met in church, did things God's way. How could he be gone after 3 years, a 1½-year-old son, and a new home purchased in November 2002? What was God's plan and why was this tragedy a part of it?

I married again on December 8, 2007. I thought the journey was over, but it was just beginning. I was married but living in fear of losing another husband. I began a journey of deliverance, but in 2010 I received a phone call from the police that my dad was found dead in his apartment. Here I stood a woman of God living in a state of anxiety and fear every day of suddenly losing someone I loved. I was ashamed and suffered an emotional breakdown. Finally, I heard the Lord say GET HELP!

In the Black community, it is often taboo to seek professional help. God assured me that He would order my steps. I began seeing a Christian counselor and a psychiatrist. I had to take medicine to function. My personal desire was not to take medicine forever, so I prayed to God to help me learn to function eventually without medicine and He did.

I BOLDLY share my journey with women I mentor to help them overcome the shame and stigma attached to therapy in the Black Community. I unapologetically declare there is no shame in seeking professional help. My mantra is PRAY, SEEK HELP & LIVE.

Letter to My Younger Self

Dear Tonya, I see you sitting in your room all alone crying because your parents are arguing again. Please stop crying and know that you did nothing wrong, and it is not your responsibility to help them stay together at the age of 12. God has not forgotten about you, and He will help you and your mom survive the emotional abuse that your dad continues to inflict on you. Don't be angry with your mom because she stayed so long, she was trying to honor the marriage vows she made before God. Your mom's focus was making sure you graduated and preparing you to be independent. You are a princess and God has a wonderful life planned for you! You don't need validation from anyone to be who God created you to be! You are fearfully and wonderfully made! BE YOU!!!

Letter to God

Dear God, Why Me? God, I know you chose me but why? Bullied as a child with low self-esteem. Emotionally abused by my dad. I considered taking the life of my dad and myself. I had 2 abortions and sometimes still can't forgive myself. I feel unworthy to be walking in your grace and mercy. I accept your forgiveness and thank you for breaking the curse of a dysfunctional family in my life!

I am a BEAUTIFUL, BOLD, BRILLIANT, BUSINESS MINDED, BLACK WOMAN who pursues what God tells me to pursue, I know my worth and value and I can do all things I purpose to do.

Write Your Own Unstoppable Letter
Dear God, Why Me?

ABOUT THE AUTHOR

Tonya Patricia Garnes Twyman was born in Henderson, North Carolina on October 14, 1966. She is a wife, mother, entrepreneur, and 31-year federal government employee. Tonya is married to the love of her life Bishop Lanier C. Twyman, Sr., Pastor of the St. Stephen Baptist Church in Temple Hills, Md. where she serves as a minister, director of Women Walking in Worship Women's Ministry, and the Co-Director of the Marriage Ministry. She is affectionately known as Lady T by their congregation and committed to ensuring that women know that God sees them no matter their circumstances. Tonya holds a Bachelor of Business Administration in Accounting from Howard University. Tonya is an Unstoppable Black Woman because through much adversity she has persevered and continued to thrive in her God-given purpose.

YOLANDA DAVIS

Unstoppable Story

I believe I am an Unstoppable Black Woman. I believe I can do all things through Christ who strengthens me. Why... because through it all, I have been resilient, steadfast, and unmovable. The naysayers, battles, and challenges come in the form of people, mindsets, and sometimes traumatic experiences. I choose to say yes to the promises of God and no to a life that does not allow me to live up to my full potential. I believe that Jesus came so that I can live more abundantly. See, for me being unstoppable manifests in my faith in God. This does not mean that I do not feel discouraged or unsure about the twists and turns of life; what it means is despite what I see and feel, I choose to press towards the goal. I believe that this great work that God began in me will not stop until it is finished. Through all of my miscarriages be it childbirth, or betrayed relationships (personal and professional), I am an unstoppable black woman. I will give out, but never will I give up on what God has for me.

Letter to My Younger Self

Girl... you have power! Your inability to manage your negative thoughts about yourself, control your emotional responses towards people, or your inability to show up as your best self, will leave you feeling powerless. When Jesus left the earth, He left you with the Holy Spirit and the ability to change how you react to the challenges in your life. The Holy Spirit is the revelation you feel when you are in the middle of a choice. Moving mountains is a figurative term for changing your mindset. What this means is you can be strategic and intentional about your presence in the world. You don't have to be what people say you are. You are who God says you are! You have the power to control your emotions by keeping a positive mindset. Decide to be anchored on the promises of God, not anything else. Choose to use your power so that you have a polished presence.

Letter to God

Dear Lord Why Me? Why, Lord, do I continue to struggle with things You delivered me from? Why, Lord, do I wrestle with negative thoughts that haunt me? Why, Lord, do I lean to my own understanding in times of trouble instead of acknowledging who You are in my life. Why is it that sometimes my joy is predicated by the actions of others, even when I know that my joy comes from You? Lord, I know You are my strength; You are my redeemer, who shall I fear. Lord, I know You are mighty, strong in battle. Why do I feel so weak? Today Lord, I am affirming to stand BOLDLY on Your promises. I am encouraged that I will have BEAUTY for my ashes. And because of the BRILLIANCE You have given me; I will continue to have a life that is abundantly BLESSED in the face of adversity.

Write Your Own Unstoppable Letter
Dear God, Why Me?

_____
_____
_____
_____
_____
_____
_____
_____
_____
_____
_____
_____
_____
_____
_____
_____
_____
_____
_____
_____
_____
_____
_____
_____
_____

ABOUT THE AUTHOR

Yolanda Davis is a certified etiquette consultant laser-focused on coaching clients on tips and strategies to develop a more polished image related to social and professional interactions. Using her exceptional people skills and professional experience of over 15 years, her clients become strategic and intentional about their personal presence in the world. Yolanda holds a Master's degree of Art in Workforce Development and Health Science Management from Webster University. She is a certified master trainer from the

Association of Training and Development and holds a Diversity, Equity, and Inclusion certificate from South Florida University. Yolanda serves as a program manager for a government agency in Washington DC. She is a beloved wife to her very supportive husband and mother of two beautiful and bold girls

www.ingramcontent.com/pod-product-compliance
Lightning Source LLC
Chambersburg PA
CBHW050652160426
43194CB00010B/1915